Copyright © [2024] [BTL Publishing].

All rights reserved. No part of this publication may be reproduced, distributed, or transmitted in any form or by any means, including photocopying, recording, or other electronic or mechanical methods, without the prior written permission of the publisher, except in the case of brief quotations embodied in critical reviews and certain other noncommercial uses permitted by copyright law.

Independently Published on Amazon KDP.

Disclaimer:

This book is an unofficial fan publication and is not authorized, endorsed, or affiliated with Billie Eilish, their management, or any related entities. All facts and opinions expressed are the author's own and are based on publicly available information.

Legal Disclaimer:

All facts presented in this book are based on publicly available information at the time of publication. Every effort has been made to ensure accuracy; however, the author does not accept responsibility for errors or omissions.

My personal
PAGE

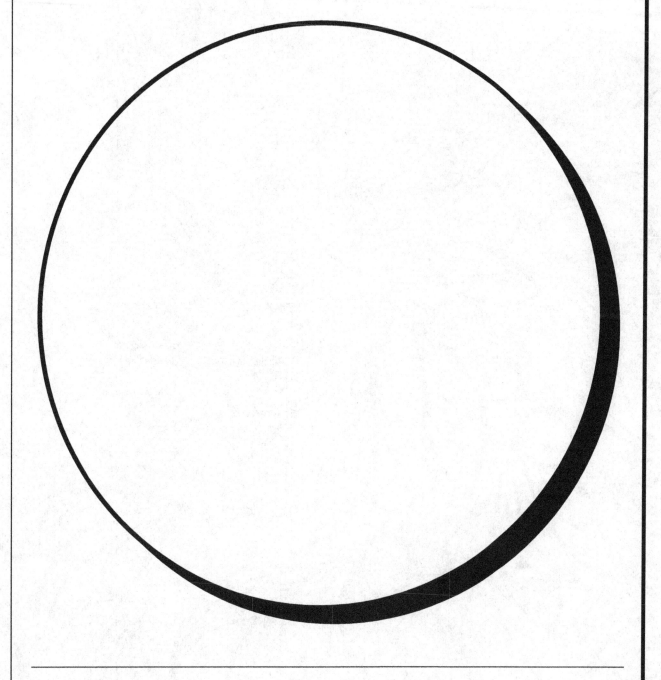

_____

_____

_____

BILLIEEILISH

Nothing ever
stops you

I`m in
love with
my
future

TRY YOUR COLORS

BEFORE COLORING, USE THIS PAGE TO TEST YOUR
MATERIALS. WITH MARKERS, PUT BLANK PAPER BEHIND
THE PAGE TO PREVENT BLEED-THROUGH.

TRY YOUR COLORS

BEFORE COLORING, USE THIS PAGE TO TEST YOUR
MATERIALS. WITH MARKERS, PUT BLANK PAPER BEHIND
THE PAGE TO PREVENT BLEED-THROUGH.

Made in the USA
Coppell, TX
08 December 2024

41969603R00050